Peace on Earth

Design by Randy McGovern

Leisure Arts Inc. • Maumelle Arkansas

How to Read the Chart

The chart is made up of a key and a gridded design where each square represents a stitch. The symbols in this key indicate the color of floss and the number of strands to use for each stitch on the chart. The following headings and symbols are given:

X — Cross Stitch
DMC — DMC color number
1/4 X — Quarter Stitch
1 strand 1/2 X — Half Cross Stitch
2 strand 1/2 X — Half Cross Stitch
B'ST — Backstitch
ANC. — Anchor color number
COLOR — the name given to the floss color in this chart

How to Stitch

Always work **Cross Stitches**, **Quarter Stitches**, and **Half Cross Stitches** first and then add the **Backstitch**.

Cross Stitch (X): For horizontal rows, work stitches in two journeys ***(Fig. 1)***. For vertical rows, complete each stitch as shown ***(Fig. 2)***.

Fig. 1

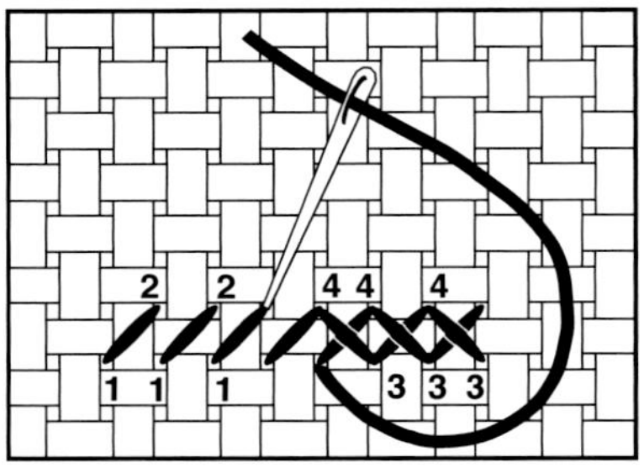

Fig. 2

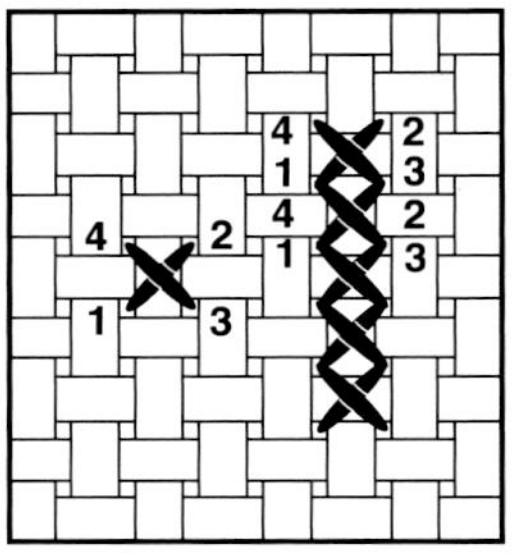

Quarter Stitch (1/4X): Come up at 1, then split fabric thread to go down at 2 ***(Fig. 3)***.

Fig. 3

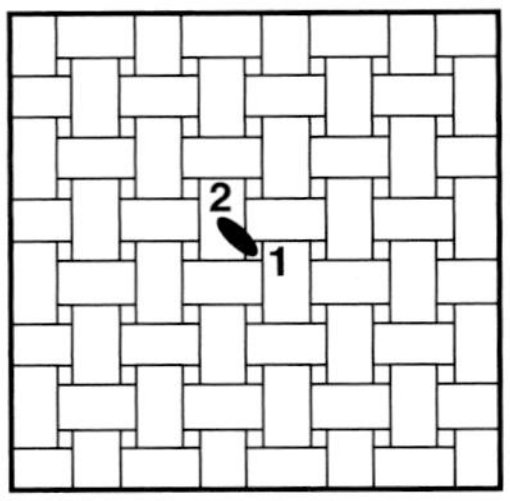

Half Cross Stitch (1/2X): This stitch is one journey of the Cross Stitch and is worked from lower left to upper right as shown in **Fig. 4**.

Fig. 4

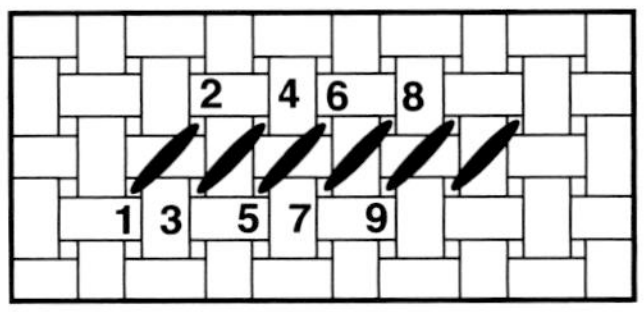

Backstitch (B'ST): For outlines and details, Backstitch should be worked after the design has been completed ***(Fig. 5)***.

Fig. 5

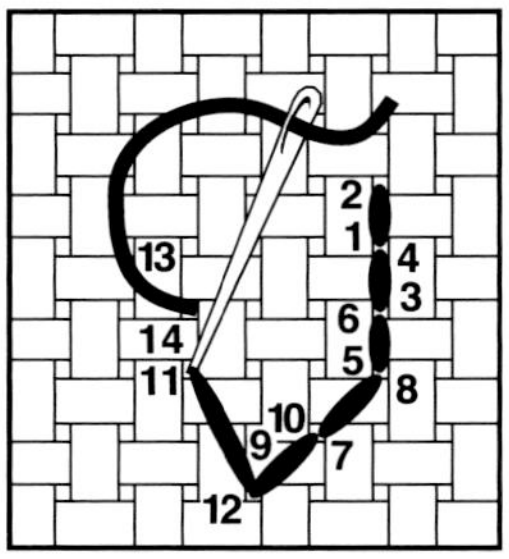

Stitching Tips

Preparing Fabric
Being sure to allow plenty of margin, cut fabric desired size and overcast raw edges. It is better to waste a little fabric than to come up short after hours of stitching!

Working with Floss
To ensure smoother stitches, separate strands and realign them before threading needle. Keep stitching tension consistent. Begin and end floss by running under several stitches on back; never tie knots.

Dye Lot Variation
It is important to buy all of the floss you need to complete your project from the same dye lot. Although variations in color may be slight when flosses from two different dye lots are held together, the variation is usually apparent on a stitched piece.

Where to Start
The horizontal and vertical centers of the charted design are shown by arrows. You may start at any point on the charted design, but be sure the design will be centered on the fabric. Locate the center of fabric by folding in half, top to bottom and again left to right. On the charted design, count the number of squares (stitches) from the center of the chart to where you wish to start. Then from the fabric's center, find your starting point by counting out the same number of fabric threads (stitches).

Peace on Earth (137w x 179h)	
14 count	9 7/8" x 12 7/8"
16 count	8 5/8" x 11 1/4"
18 count	7 5/8" x 10"

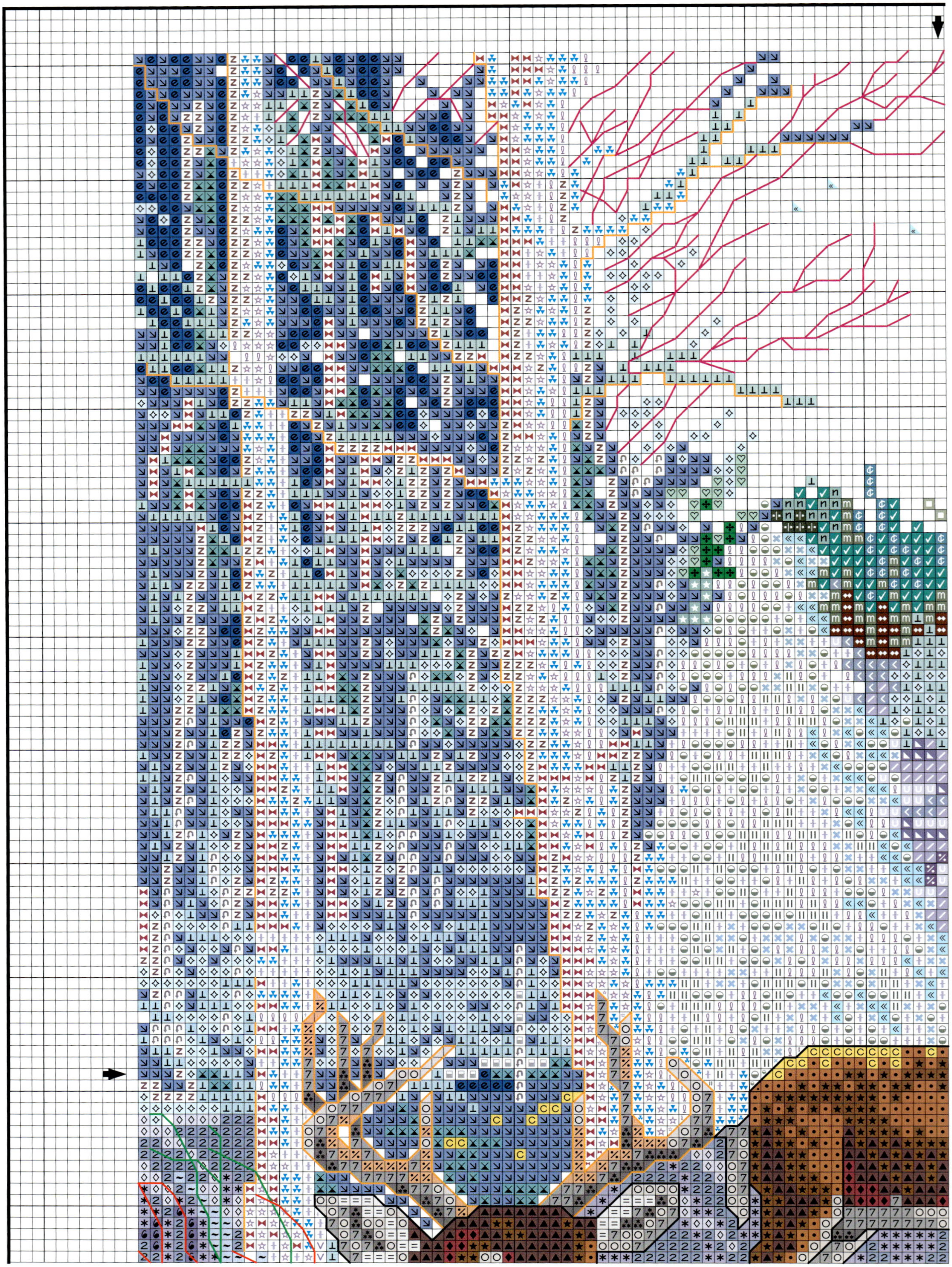

PEACE ON EARTH (137w x 179h)

X	DMC	1/4X	1 strand 1/2X	2 strand 1/2X	B'ST	ANC.	COLOR
	310					403	black
	420					374	dk gold
	422				*	943	lt gold
	640					903	taupe
*	640					903	taupe
	642					392	lt taupe
*	642					392	lt taupe
	644					830	vy lt taupe
	794					175	blue
*	794					175	blue
†	[794 3051					175 681	blue green
	822					390	beige
	869					944	vy dk gold
	924					851	dk teal
	926					850	lt teal
*	935					861	dk green
	938					381	brown
	3021					905	vy dk taupe
*	3021					905	vy dk taupe
†	[3021 3865				°	905	vy dk taupe winter white
	3045				*	888	gold
†	[3045 3865					888	gold winter white
*	3051					681	green
	3052					262	lt green
†	[3052 3747					262 120	lt green vy lt blue
*	3747					120	vy lt blue
	3756					1037	baby blue
*	3756					1037	baby blue

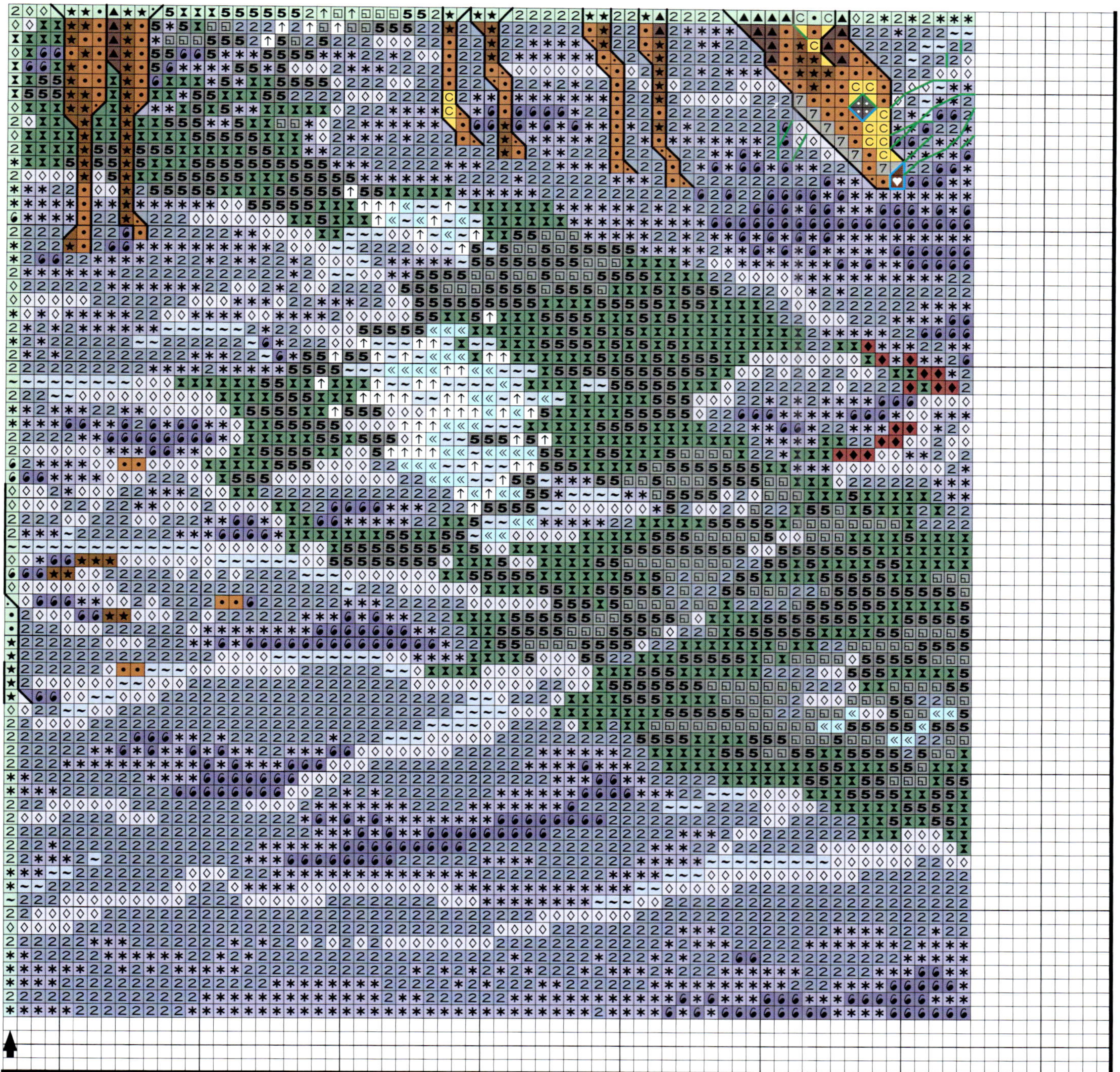

X	DMC	1/4X	1 strand 1/2X	2 strand 1/2X	B'ST	ANC.	COLOR
5	3768	◩				779	teal
▲	3790	◩		∾		393	dk taupe
Z*	3790					393	dk taupe
† [	3790			¢		393	dk taupe
	3839						dk blue
6	3807	◩		◣		122	denim
✱	3838	◩	e	◩			vy dk blue
V*	3838						vy dk blue
2	3839	◩	⊠	<			dk blue
☆*	3839	◩					dk blue
~	3840	◩	⊥	%	◩ ○		lt blue
+*	3840	◩					lt blue
«† [	3865	◩					winter white
	Kreinik blending filament 032						pearl
↑	5283						silver metallic floss
	Green areas indicate last row of previous section of design.						

* Use **1** strand of floss.

† Use **1** strand of each floss color listed.

★ DMC 422 for deer. DMC 3045 for grass.

○ DMC 3021/3865 for trees and limbs. DMC 3840 for snow line and deer.

Peace on Earth was stitched on a 16" x 19" piece of 14 count Navy Aida (design size 9 7/8" x 12 7/8"). Two strands of floss were used for Cross Stitch and 1 strand for Backstitch unless noted in key. It was custom framed.

Show us what you're working on!

Share your project photos with us on social media.
Tag us @leisureartsinc or use #leisurearts

Production Team: Writer – Mimi Harrington; Artist – Crystal Hastings; and Photo Stylist – Karen Hall.

Fabric provided courtesy of Charles Craft, Inc.
Embroidery floss provided courtesy of The DMC Corporation.

Instructions tested and photo model made by Anne Simpson.

Made in U.S.A.